FEMA Strategic Plan
Fiscal Years 2011-2014

FEMA P-806 / February 2011

 FEMA

Administrator's Foreword

★ ★ ★

FEMA's mission is to support our citizens and first responders to ensure that as a nation we work together to build, sustain, and improve our capability to prepare for, protect against, respond to, recover from, and mitigate all hazards. To help us stay focused on this mission, I am pleased to present FEMA's 2011 – 2014 Strategic Plan. This plan continues the strategic direction as described in the Administrator's Intent 2012 – 2016. It identifies specific initiatives that we will accomplish over the next several years that will significantly enhance the Nation's security and resilience and our ability to serve our vital role as a member of the Nation's emergency management team.

FEMA's strategic plan is consistent with the Agency's history and culture, as described in our capstone doctrine, FEMA Publication 1. We have been, and will continue to be, an organization that is growing, evolving, and adapting to changing conditions and demands on our services. This plan recognizes that FEMA will need to remain a flexible organization that continues to adapt to the future environment, while at the same time remaining faithful to our ethos of *"serving the Nation by helping its people and first responders, especially when they are most in need."* This plan demonstrates the application of our ethos and core values and, as such, it is an important statement about who we are as an agency and our mission focus.

Prior to the development of this strategic plan, the FEMA leadership team sought to address current and future challenges facing the organization. At a Senior Leadership conference in December 2009, the leadership team identified three initiatives for 2010 designed to focus FEMA actions on tackling challenges of long-term importance: (1) Developing a new framework for catastrophic planning that focuses on stabilizing an event within 72 hours and recognizes that the public is the most important partner on the emergency management team; (2) instituting workforce enhancement that will ensure FEMA employees are fully trained and equipped to perform their mission; and (3) the creation of capstone doctrine for FEMA (FEMA Publication 1) that provides the context for the implementation of this strategic plan. These initiatives represented a strategic focus on priorities that are critical to FEMA's long-term success. FEMA has made demonstrable progress on all 2010 initiatives: Completing FEMA's Publication 1; implementing work force development initiatives such as a new performance rating system and the Mission Readiness course that establishes a comprehensive employee orientation program; and designing and implementing a new planning framework for catastrophic disaster response. Despite this progress, much work remains to be done.

FEMA recognizes that we are only one member of a broad national emergency management team—one that includes Federal, state, local, tribal, and territorial governments, the private sector, non-governmental organizations, faith-based and community-based organizations, and the American public. Further, the Agency acknowledges that the rapid pace of change in the world cannot be controlled and that the conditions we operate within will continue to evolve. At the same time, experience has taught us that we must do a better job of providing services for the entire community, regardless of their background, demographics, or challenges. This means planning for the actual makeup of a community, and making sure we meet the needs of every disaster survivor regardless of age, economics, or accessibility requirements.

Addressing these related concerns cannot be achieved by simply improving on what we have always done – we must fundamentally change how we go about disaster preparedness, response, recovery and mitigation, involving the communities we serve directly in these efforts. We must look beyond the traditional, government-centric approach to emergency management and embrace a philosophy and operational posture that leverages, and serves, the Whole Community.

This strategic plan advances a Whole Community approach to the practice of emergency management that embraces the reality that it takes all aspects of a community (volunteer, faith and community-based organizations, the private sector, and the public, including survivors themselves) – not just the government – to effectively prepare for, protect against, respond to, recover from, and mitigate against any disaster. It builds upon the aforementioned 2010 initiatives by strengthening engagement among emergency managers and the communities they serve, and integrates new partners and new approaches to build the Nation's capacity to manage catastrophic disasters, foster a common understanding of the risks we face as a national emergency management team, and advance solutions that engage the Whole Community in every aspect of emergency management. Finally, this strategic plan will assist in creating a more flexible and agile FEMA, which will allow the Agency to adapt to new challenges and take advantage of new opportunities in a rapidly changing world.

We will dedicate the resources necessary to accomplish the initiatives described within this strategic plan. I expect all FEMA personnel to read our strategic plan and commit to its implementation. Whether directly engaged in these initiatives or in supporting efforts, everyone working for FEMA must understand the intent and philosophy behind the initiatives and use them as a guide in the performance of their duties. Furthermore, FEMA will engage and partner with the Nation's emergency management team to accomplish the goals and initiatives that cannot succeed without their support. It is my strong belief that these initiatives will enhance the practice of emergency management in the United States, strengthen the Nation's resilience to disasters, and make FEMA a more effective organization now and for the future.

W. Craig Fugate
Administrator

Table of Contents

★ ★ ★

Introduction

★ ★ ★

The past three decades have presented the emergency management community with significant challenges and conditions that have necessitated reevaluation of strategic and operational approaches to delivering emergency management services. To address those challenges, FEMA recognizes that the emergency management community must operate as a team, which underscores the Agency's mission: *to support our citizens and first responders to ensure that as a Nation we work together to build, sustain, and improve our capability to prepare for, protect against, respond to, recover from, and mitigate all hazards*. FEMA is only one member of the broad national emergency management team—one that includes Federal, state, local, tribal, and territorial governments, private sector, nongovernmental organizations, faith-based and community-based organizations, and the American public. We know that the rapid pace of change in the world provides opportunities to strengthen emergency management, and that conditions will continuously evolve and affect every aspect of society. These factors mean FEMA must work with the public, our most important partner, as well as our traditional and many new partners, to innovate and test new ways to achieve critical outcomes.

This strategic plan was developed with an understanding of contemporary practices,

> *"We're going to succeed as a team, or we're going to fail as a team: even if FEMA does everything right, we can't succeed without the team."*
>
> **-W. Craig Fugate, Administrator**

lessons from past experience, and an appreciation for what the future may bring. The FEMA 2011–2014 initiatives will make FEMA a more flexible and adaptive organization capable of responding to new situations, capitalizing on opportunities, and quickly adjusting to changing environments. The initiatives will foster greater community engagement, and unity of effort and purpose among all members of the emergency management team, with the goal of achieving more effective emergency management outcomes for the Nation.

FEMA's 2011–2014 Initiatives

1. Foster a Whole Community Approach to Emergency Management Nationally

2. Build the Nation's Capacity to Stabilize and Recover From a Catastrophic Event

3. Build Unity of Effort and Common Strategic Understanding Among the Emergency Management Team

4. Enhance FEMA's Ability to Learn and Innovate as an Organization

The Future Strategic Environment

★★★

An assessment of the conditions that will shape the next ten to twenty years reveals challenges and opportunities for FEMA and the emergency management community. While there are many uncertain dynamics facing the Nation, broad themes are emerging that are especially important to the Agency and the field of emergency management: Increased empowerment of individuals due to technological innovation; the evolving security environment; dramatic demographic shifts; and changes in the manmade and natural environments.

Rapid innovations in technology, the transformation of the information environment and the impact of these developments on how individuals relate to society in general—and government in particular—will create both challenges and opportunities for emergency management. Significant trends include an increase in "spontaneous reporting" where individuals at or near an incident instantly post video, images, and messages from their personal communications devices. Spontaneous reporting has the potential to enhance our collective situational awareness considerably by integrating information provided by the public with that provided from official government and other unofficial sources. Increased technology also has potential to confuse decision making during a crisis situation if it is misunderstood or discounted. The increasing avail-

ability of multiple sources of information will place a premium on the ability of government officials to communicate with and through trusted information sources, and challenges the effectiveness of traditional communications methods. These trends, along with the development of virtual communities, in addition to geographic, institutional, faith, and interest-based communities, will continue to shift influence away from formal, institutional-based governance structures and more toward individuals and groups.

The evolving terrorist threat combined with ever increasing global interdependencies will create a fluctuating national and international security situation. The availability of technological and scientific knowledge has the potential to transform both terrorist and counterterrorist capabilities while the rapidly evolving information environment continues to create avenues for individuals and small groups to seek out and associate with extremists. America's reliance on an increasingly vulnerable global supply chain and shifting international political and economic power dynamics may also mean that catastrophes abroad have a greater impact domestically.

Several anticipated dramatic demographic shifts are shaping the location and composition of the American public. The United States has more people living in more vul-

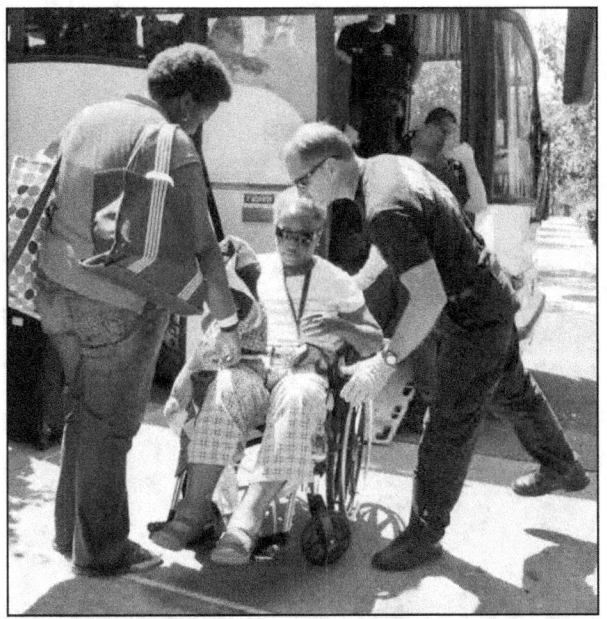

A Corpus Christi firefighter assists a resident who uses a wheel chair into a bus. Source: FEMA Photo Library

Urban Search and Rescue teams discuss rescue efforts in Louisiana with a FEMA public information officer. Source: FEMA Photo Library

nerable areas than ever before. There will also be a significant increase in the elderly population, those over the age of sixty-five, as well as a continued diversification of America's population. These trends will create new medical, cultural, and linguistic challenges that must be addressed in emergency management planning, response, and recovery. The fastest growing areas of the country are large metropolitan areas, particularly the suburbs outside major urban areas. As metropolitan areas continue to grow, an increase in development in more vulnerable locations, such as flood plains and coastal regions, will also likely continue.

Changes to both the manmade and natural environments also have the potential to impact FEMA's operating environment significantly. For example, much of the country's critical infrastructure is nearing the end of its life-cycle and may require significant investment to prevent a crisis. Collapsing bridges, weakening dams, bursting water mains, overburdened health and medical systems, and a fragile power grid are all examples of this well documented situation. Without reliable infrastructure in place, protection, response, and recovery will become more difficult. Further, challenges posed by climate change, such as more intense storms, frequent heavy precipitation, heat waves, drought, extreme flooding, and higher sea levels, have the potential to change significantly the types and magnitudes of hazards faced by communities and the emergency management professionals serving them. Taken together, the challenges of deteriorating infrastructure and the effects of climate change will exacerbate one another's impacts, furthering the challenge to the emergency management community.

The implications of the future environment require FEMA and the entire emergency management community to engage with citizens as our most powerful partners; to use emerging technologies; to plan for an older and more diverse population; to understand the implications of new weapons, tactics, and intent of terrorists; and to appreciate the risks posed by aging infrastructure and a changing climate. Understanding this future environment will enable FEMA to adjust its current approach and strategies to navigate the future successfully.

Understanding Future Strategic Needs

To better understand how emergency management might be affected by future changes in the world, FEMA launched a Strategic Foresight Initiative (SFI). Working with emergency management partners at all levels of government, as well as the private sector and academia, FEMA considered nine drivers of change that will likely affect emergency management. These drivers were:

- The changing role of the individual;

- Climate change;

- The age of critical infrastructure;

- Evolving terrorist threats;

- Global interdependencies;

- Government budgets;

- Technical innovation and dependency;

- Universal access to and use of information; and

- U.S. demographic shifts.

Figure 1—Strategic Foresight Initiative

FEMA Hazard Mitigation Specialists discuss options for protecting a water treatment plant in Nashville with a local official. Source: FEMA Photo Library

Cars and roadway at the site of the I-35 bridge collapse in Minneapolis. Source: FEMA Photo Library

FEMA's Approach and Strategic Context

★ ★ ★

As FEMA continues to adapt and develop innovative ways to provide better emergency management services in light of the changing environment, the Agency must stay true to its core values and guiding principles: compassion, fairness, integrity, and respect. This strategic plan leverages FEMA's values and applies them to a set of practices that focus on the achievement of key outcomes in priority areas.

Based on the Agency's core values and guiding principles (Figure 2), FEMA leadership established five priorities designed to address the Agency's current and future challenges. The Agency's leadership sought to delineate FEMA Headquarters as the source of operational and strategic guidance, while looking to the FEMA Regions to manage resources and implement the strategic direction. The Priorities, articulated in the Administrator's Statement of Intent for FY 2012 - 2016, further build on this desire to empower the FEMA Regions.

- First, FEMA must strengthen the Nation's resilience to disasters. FEMA must enable individuals, families, and communities to withstand disruption, absorb or tolerate disturbance, act effectively in a crisis, adapt to changing conditions, and grow stronger over time.

- Second, FEMA must build unity of effort among the entire emergency manage-

Core Values

Compassion
Fairness
Integrity
Respect

Guiding Principles

Teamwork
Engagement
Getting Results
Preparation
Empowerment
Flexibility
Accountability
Stewardship

Figure 2—Core Values/Guiding Principles

ment team through clearly defined roles and responsibilities for communities and individuals, access to information, and a shared understanding of how risks are managed and prioritized.

- Third, FEMA must effectively support the needs of disaster survivors and the recovery of affected communities.

- Fourth, FEMA must work with its partners to address our most significant risks. Accepting that risk cannot be totally eliminated, it is essential to develop a common understanding of the risks responders and communities face, and

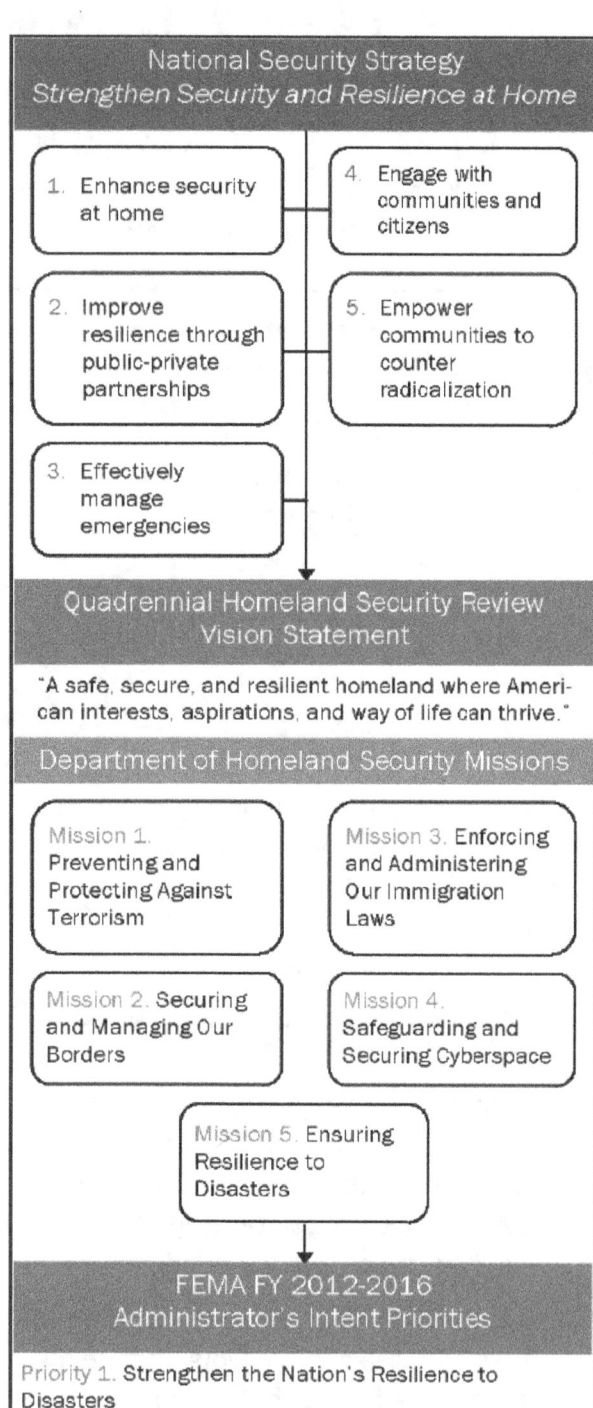

National Security Strategy
Strengthen Security and Resilience at Home

1. Enhance security at home

2. Improve resilience through public-private partnerships

3. Effectively manage emergencies

4. Engage with communities and citizens

5. Empower communities to counter radicalization

Quadrennial Homeland Security Review
Vision Statement

"A safe, secure, and resilient homeland where American interests, aspirations, and way of life can thrive."

Department of Homeland Security Missions

Mission 1. Preventing and Protecting Against Terrorism

Mission 2. Securing and Managing Our Borders

Mission 3. Enforcing and Administering Our Immigration Laws

Mission 4. Safeguarding and Securing Cyberspace

Mission 5. Ensuring Resilience to Disasters

FEMA FY 2012-2016
Administrator's Intent Priorities

Priority 1. Strengthen the Nation's Resilience to Disasters
Priority 2. Build Unity of Effort Among the Entire Emergency Management Team
Priority 3. Meet the Needs of Disaster Survivors and Effectively Support the Recovery of Disaster-Affected Communities
Priority 4. Work with Our Partners to Address Our Most Significant Risks
Priority 5. Build, Sustain, and Improve FEMA's Mission Support and Workforce Capabilities

Figure 3— FEMA Strategic Context

to plan, understand preparedness gaps, and build capabilities together to address those of highest collective concern.

- Fifth, FEMA must build, sustain, and improve its workforce and develop its current and future leadership. People are the backbone of any organization and FEMA is no exception. FEMA staff must have the tools they need to accomplish the mission. FEMA's ability to develop its workforce is the single most important driver of the Agency's future success.

The FEMA Strategic Plan is part of a broader strategic framework to enhance both national and homeland security in the United States through coordinated action by the Federal government. This strategy links to, and supports, the President's National Security Strategy (NSS), the Department of Homeland Security's Quadrennial Homeland Security Review (QHSR), DHS missions, and the priorities expressed in the FEMA Administrator's Intent, as shown in Figure 3. This strategic context, as reflected in the FEMA Strategic Plan, ensures FEMA's actions are both aligned with and support the President's and Secretary of Homeland Security's strategic objectives.

The 2011-2014 strategic initiatives articulated in this plan have been shaped by FEMA's core values, our history, and a pragmatic look at what the future may bring. They support the President's ultimate goal of "Strengthening Security and Resilience at Home" as reflected in the National Security Strategy, as well as the goals established for the Department of Homeland Security's

An emergency manager from the Virgin Islands gives FEMA and local emergency workers a situational briefing about impending hurricanes. Source: FEMA Photo Library

"Ensuring Resilience to Disasters" mission and the Administrator's Intent Priorities.

The following 2011-2014 strategic initiatives (Figure 4) draw on the strategic context to provide direction on how FEMA will advance community engagement in emergency management, build the Nation's capacity to withstand catastrophic disasters, foster a common understanding of risk, and increase FEMA's flexibility and agility.

FEMA's 2011-2014 Initiatives

Initiative 1: Foster a Whole Community Approach to Emergency Management Nationally

Initiative 2: Build the Nation's Capacity to Stabilize and Recover From a Catastrophic Event

Initiative 3: Build Unity of Effort and Common Strategic Understanding Among the Emergency Management Team

Initiative 4: Enhance FEMA's Ability to Learn and Innovate as an Organization

Figure 4—FEMA's 2011–2014 Initiatives

Initiative 1

★ ★ ★

Foster a Whole Community Approach to Emergency Management Nationally

FEMA recognizes that it takes all aspects of a community (volunteer, faith, and community-based organizations, the private sector, and the public, including survivors themselves) – not just the government – to effectively prepare for, protect against, respond to, recover from, and mitigate against any disaster. It is therefore critical that we work together to enable communities to develop collective, mutually supporting local capabilities to withstand the potential initial impacts of these events, respond quickly, and recover in a way that sustains or improves the community's overall well-being. How communities achieve this collective capacity calls for innovative approaches – from across the full spectrum of community actors, including emergency management – to expand and enhance existing practices, institutions, and organizations that help make local communities successful every day, under normal conditions, and leverage this social infrastructure to help meet community needs when an incident occurs.

Emergency managers have historically focused on managing the impacts of disasters, both before and after they occur. While these efforts are essential, they represent only one end of a broad continuum of actions that build sustainable and resilient communities. At the other end of this continuum are activities that focus on the development, health, and long-term success of those communities. For example, by strengthening underlying community conditions disaster resilience can be improved.

Source: FEMA Photo Library

Activities that aim to provide good jobs, expand housing and transportation choices, plan for future community development, or improve energy sustainability can also provide direct and indirect benefits that enhance disaster resilience. Applying the core competencies of emergency management – communicating, coordinating, and collaborating – to engaging with the many groups and organizations that are already working in these and other areas is key to building the capacity of American society to be resilient. Communities will organize themselves to deal with crises in much the same way as they organize to deal with daily challenges. By working together with new partners and focusing on strengthening what works well in communities on a daily basis, we can advance creative solutions that build collective Whole Community disaster management capabilities and help strengthen the Nation's resilience.

The ways in which individuals and communities engage with each other and with government are changing. The NSS and the QHSR recognize community engagement as a foundational principle for strengthening national preparedness and resilience. This will require emergency managers at all levels to engage proactively with businesses, neighborhood associations, community groups, faith-based and community-based organizations, ethnic centers, and other civic-minded organizations that have routine, direct ties and established trust with the individuals who live in their communities, and that can mobilize their networks to build community resilience and support local emergency management needs.

Americorps members at a Missouri church unload a truckload of beds donated to survivors of a tornado. Source: FEMA Photo Library

FEMA's approach seeks to work with the state, local, tribal, and territorial governments to encourage emergency managers at all levels to engage more effectively with and support local communities in activities that, directly or indirectly, build preparedness and resilience. The aim is to foster development of a community-oriented model for emergency management that emphasizes understanding community complexity and how social activity is organized on a "normal" basis and planning for the actual makeup of our communities. This means building partnerships to engage effectively with the full spectrum of community residents and members (including but not limited to people speaking diverse languages or from diverse cultures or economic backgrounds, all ages from children and youth to seniors, people with disabilities, others with access and functional needs, and populations traditionally underrepresented in civic governance), realigning emergency management practices to support local needs, and working to strengthen the institutions, assets, and networks that work well in communities on a daily basis. The core proposition underlying this ap-

> *"We need to move away from the mindset that Federal and State governments are always in the lead, and build upon the strengths of our local communities and, more importantly, our citizens. We must treat individuals and communities as key assets rather than liabilities."*
>
> **-W. Craig Fugate, Administrator**

proach is that resilience depends on the success of collective action and local institutions before an incident. A Whole Community model that works to strengthen local collective action, public engagement, and neighborhood institutions offers an effective path not only to building resilience, but to helping local communities become integral members of the emergency management team.

Additionally, FEMA will establish partnerships with foundations and community-based organizations that can act as third-party intermediaries and encourage local communities to engage in creative activities that enhance disaster resilience by building

on and addressing local needs. Working through these partnerships, FEMA will assist in the implementation of programs designed to stimulate, support, and expand the scale of existing, successful community activities and to encourage local residents to design new collaborative initiatives that will enhance community resilience.

Through these activities, FEMA seeks to spark dramatic expansion and transformation of current community engagement strategies in the field of emergency management, promoting approaches that position local residents in leadership roles in planning, organizing, and sharing accountability for the success of local disaster management efforts. We believe that Whole Community Emergency Management is a philosophy that should be applied to everything we do as an agency and as a field of practice. To that end, FEMA will lead the development of guidance, tools, training, and educational programs to enable effective engagement and integration of the entire community into local emergency management activities to strengthen resilience and improve outcomes.

Key Outcomes to Achieve

- Institutionalize mainstream emergency management practices nationally that focus on strengthening local institutions, assets, and social networks as a path to building resilience

- Create a collective body of knowledge among the emergency management team nationally that supports a Whole Community approach to emergency management

- Successfully seed innovative, grassroots resilience-building activities in communities across the country

Initiative 2

★ ★ ★

Build the Nation's Capacity to Stabilize and Recover From a Catastrophic Event

The Nation's emergency management system works well for small- to moderate-scale disasters; but the real challenges lie in preparing for an unprecedented catastrophic event where the human, materiel, and financial effects exceed current response and recovery capabilities. If the emergency management community cannot mobilize governmental, private, and civic sector resources within and outside of the affected area in a coordinated and timely manner, then the nation cannot hope to respond effectively. The first 72 hours following a catastrophe are critical, and our ability, as a Nation, to stabilize the affected area is key to saving and sustaining lives, and enabling delivery of an effective response. Once life-saving and life-sustaining operations have ceased, it is equally important to rapidly restore basic services and community functionality. As the stabilization process unfolds, and communities seek to recover and help build a more resilient nation, all recovery partners must operate in a unified and collaborative manner to restore, redevelop and revitalize the social, structural, economic, and natural environment and systems.

Through what is termed as the "Maximum of Maximums" framework for catastrophic planning, FEMA has begun an initiative focused on adopting a Whole Community approach to address these three challenges: building the Nation's capability to stabilize a catastrophic event in the first 72 hours, re-

Source: FEMA Photo Library

storing basic services and community functionality within 60 days, and building the Nation's capability to support recovery from the long-term effects of the event within five years. FEMA's approach involves first defining the critical outcomes that must be achieved to realize these objectives (Figure 5). FEMA will work with private industry, faith-based and community-based organizations, civic sector, nongovernmental, and community development partners in state, local, tribal and territorial governments to look at new ways of doing business and to design innovative approaches to achieving these outcomes. These approaches will be tested through National Level Exercises, and codified in national planning documents, concepts of operation, protocols, and agreements. Throughout this effort, FEMA will embrace a whole community approach, emphasizing that individuals and communities are our most critical response and recovery assets during the initial hours and days, and even years, following an event. FEMA will also actively engage all sectors of society in participatory planning and preparedness activities.

For the first phase of this initiative, the 72 hour response phase, FEMA commenced work in FY 2010 on developing the critical core capabilities necessary for both saving and sustaining lives and stabilizing the site impacted by a catastrophic event, the achievement of which cannot be realized through current solutions. The second phase of the initiative focuses on the restoration of basic services and community functionality, within 60 days after the conclusion of life-saving and life-sustaining op-

Core Capabilities for Stabilization and Restoration

Enable Response:
- Situational Assessment
- Public Messaging
- Command, Control, and Coordination
- Critical Communications
- Environmental Health and Safety Critical Transportation

Survivor Needs:
- On-Scene Security and Protection
- Mass Search and Rescue Operations
- Health and Medical Treatment
- Mass Care Services
- Public and Private Services and Resources
- Stabilize and Repair Essential Infrastructure
- Fatality Management Services

Restoration:
- Essential Service Facilities
- Utilities
- Transportation Routes
- Schools
- Neighborhood Retail Businesses
- Offices and Other Workplaces

Figure 5—Core Capabilities

erations. Restoration of basic services and community functionality in this context means restoring meaningful operating capacity for essential city service facilities, utilities, transportation routes, schools, neighborhood retail businesses, and offices and other workplaces. This does not presume that every such facility or system would be reopened, or that they would be operating at 100 percent of pre-disaster levels, but that these critical systems would be back on line and local commerce would be returning. For example, not every school may be open or operating on a normal schedule, but the school system would be operating and able to accommodate the needs of children in the affected area through temporary measures. As with the development of national capability to stabilize a catastrophic event, solutions to restore basic services and community functionality will require new approaches and engagement with new partners to create conceptual and operational models to support the achievement of this set of critical outcomes and weave the results into future training, exercises, and evaluation.

The third phase of the initiative focuses on recovery within five years of the event. Recovery in this context means: achieving the goals, benchmarks, and metrics as established in the aftermath of the disaster by the local jurisdiction. This may mean the complete redevelopment and revitalization of the impacted area, rebuilding or relocating damaged or destroyed social, economic, natural and built environments and a move to self-sufficiency, sustainability and resilience. Recovery encompasses more than the restoration of a community's physical structures to their pre-disaster conditions. Of equal importance is providing a continuum of care to meet the needs of community members who have experienced the hardships of financial, emotional and/or physical impacts as well as positioning the community to meet the needs of the future. Meeting these needs — through strengthening the health and human services, social fabric, housing and educational systems, environmental sustainability and cultural resources — serves to enhance the overall resiliency of the entire community as the

Relief supplies for survivors of Hurricane Alex are checked into a FEMA staging area. Source: FEMA Photo Library

FEMA supply trailers containing generators, food, and water are staged before a hurricane in North Carolina. Source: FEMA Photo Library

A Mobile Disaster Recovery Center Vehicle provides telecommunication services for disaster response in a Georgia community. Source: FEMA Photo Library

> *"In the event of a terrorist attack, natural disaster, or other large-scale emergency, the Department and FEMA provide a coordinated, comprehensive federal response and work with Federal, state, local, and private sector partners to ensure a swift and effective recovery effort. Working together, we continue to build a ready and resilient nation by providing grants and training to our partners, coordinating the federal government's response to disasters, and streamlining rebuilding and recovery along the Gulf Coast and throughout the Nation."*
>
> **-Janet Napolitano, Secretary of the Department of Homeland Security**

recovery progresses. As with the development of the response and stabilization capabilities for a catastrophic event, solutions to assist communities to recover will require new approaches and engagement with new partners to achieve critical outcomes.

Additionally, in support of these larger objectives, FEMA will improve the capacity and readiness of its own operational elements. The Agency will continue to identify and promulgate doctrine to provide guidance and standardization for the execution of its missions. FEMA will establish a dynamic readiness measurement system that can provide near-real time visibility into the operational status and capability of FEMA teams and deployable assets. FEMA will also implement a credentialing and qualifications system for all FEMA operational personnel. FEMA Headquarters will empower the Regions by ensuring the Regions have the guidance, staff, funding and other resources required to implement FEMA programs. These efforts will enhance FEMA's own operational capabilities, ensuring a timely, capable, professional response.

Key Outcomes to Achieve

- Establish a national capability to treat, stabilize, and provide care for 265,000 casualties following a catastrophic event

- Establish a national capability to move and distribute materiel and supplies to meet the needs of 1.5 million disaster survivors within 72 hours

- Establish a national capability to restore and sustain basic services and community functionality for an affected area of seven million people within 60 days

- Establish a national capability to recover the communities of 1.5 million disaster survivors within 5 years of the event

- Implement a performance-based qualification requirements system for all FEMA personnel participating in disaster response and recovery activities and a dynamic readiness measurement system for FEMA teams and deployable assets

Initiative 3

★ ★ ★

Build Unity of Effort and Common Strategic Understanding Among the Emergency Management Team

The Nation must prepare for, protect against, respond to, recover from, and mitigate numerous risks to the health and welfare of the American people. It is essential to develop a common understanding of risk to effectively plan, assess gaps, mitigate, and build capabilities to address risk-based requirements. The emergency management team needs to focus on those issues that challenge the national response capabilities. Addressing these risks effectively requires unity of effort and joint planning and actions across the distributed emergency management enterprise, including FEMA, its Regions, and all of its partners— other Federal agencies and state, local,

tribal and territorial governments, private industry, non-governmental organizations, faith- and community-based organizations, and the public. This, in turn, necessitates that we build shared context and understanding with our partners of the severity of the challenges we face. Based on this shared understanding, we can then work together to set priorities jointly and design solutions that address these challenges so that we may act with unity of purpose and achieve concrete outcomes that benefit the safety and welfare of all citizens.

To this end, FEMA and its Regions will engage with key private sector, State, local,

Source: FEMA Photo Library

Threat and Hazard Identification and Risk Assessments

Called for in the September 2010 report to Congress by the Local, State, Tribal, and Federal Preparedness Task Force, Threat and Hazard Identification and Risk Assessments (THIRAs) are intended to be tools that allow organizations at all levels of government to identify, assess, and prioritize their natural and man-made risks. These assessments are meant to facilitate the identification of capability and resource gaps, and allow organizations to track their year-to-year progress to address those gaps. THIRAs should leverage existing hazard mitigation processes, but be conducted in a reasonably standard manner so that results may be incorporated into Federal-level assessments.

Figure 6—Threat and Hazard Identification and Risk Assessment

and Tribal risk managers, and non-governmental partners to identify the top threats and hazards—and opportunities—in each FEMA region (Figure 6). As a partner in this effort, FEMA will share its own analyses and perceptions of risk, and will be open to the perspectives of others. Through this exchange, a composite picture of risk will be developed in each FEMA region that is reflective of the diverse views and priorities of all members of the emergency management team—public, private, and civic. FEMA, working through its regional offices, will develop regional planning assumptions that align with the critical outcomes necessary to stabilize and restore basic services and community functionality following a catastrophic event based on the unique risks and shared challenges in each region.

FEMA will work with our partners to identify and implement priority actions and new solutions that will address these regional planning assumptions, leveraging the full range of emergency management activities including preparedness, mitigation, response, and pre-incident recovery planning. In particular, FEMA will seek out opportunities to

A FEMA Federal Coordinating Officer and emergency manager work to identify risks to the All American Canal. Source: FEMA Photo Library

FEMA mitigation surveyors review a list of Repetitive Loss properties they are surveying. Source: FEMA Photo Library

"design in" resilience-building activities. These activities may include working to integrate disaster management approaches more fully into community planning and development processes; fostering adoption and enforcement of resilient building codes; engaging private industry, nongovernmental organizations, and

A home being elevated to comply with new requirements for homes being built or repaired in the area devastated during Hurricane Ike. Source: FEMA Photo Library

the public in operational planning activities and capability building; and strengthening capacities for local collective action in our communities, thus yielding better overall mitigation and response efforts. FEMA will also work with our Federal, state, local, tribal and territorial partners to enhance and maximize the use of existing technologies and communications pathways to share risk information transparently with private industry, nongovernmental organizations, local communities, and the public.

Key Outcomes to Achieve

- Conduct Regional Threat and Hazard Identification and Risk Assessments (THIRA) in each FEMA Region, in coordination with members of the emergency management team. These assessments should: (a) reflect the vital interests and priorities of each partner; and (b) contain tailored regional planning assumptions based on the threats and risks present in each region

- Develop joint action plans to address regional planning assumptions for response and recovery in each FEMA Region

- Facilitate the adoption and enforcement, where feasible and appropriate, of building codes and other protection and mitigation activities at the State level that enhance resilience to the risks identified in the Regional THIRAs, address energy sustainability, and ensure universal design of buildings, transportation vehicles, etc. to meet the access and functional needs of all individuals

Initiative 4

★★★

Enhance FEMA's Ability to Learn and Innovate as an Organization

The operational realities of crises make it impossible to predict exactly who is going to be doing what, when, why, and/or how in a disaster environment. This initiative puts a premium on developing organizational capacity to learn from past experience, rapidly orient and apply that learning in current contexts, and adapt to quickly changing conditions. FEMA can facilitate this kind of organizational growth by improving its evaluation of operational performance in both real world incidents and simulated exercises.

FEMA will develop an integrated after action review process to evaluate operational performance in both real and simulated events consistently. FEMA will then work with our partners to track efforts to act on and address lessons learned. FEMA's methodology will be nimble and support the rapid analysis of raw data and have mechanisms that allow for the near-real time sharing of after action findings with partners within and outside of government. The methodology will also be performance-based, allowing for comparisons between predicted and actual performance and incorporating meta analyses that look across multiple events and exercises to analyze performance trends over time. FEMA's approach will seek to develop a broader understanding of national capabilities and readiness that transcends the particulars of individual incidents or scenarios, and will include analyses of how underlying community conditions

Source: FEMA Photo Library

and vulnerabilities may have contributed to outcomes experienced in disasters. In doing so, the evaluation process will provide a mechanism used to engage with new partners to strengthen disaster resilience. Consistently evaluating operational performance and acting on lessons learned will better enable FEMA and the emergency management community to share best practices and implement effective ideas and solutions, thus creating an emergency management culture that positively evolves as a

A FEMA officer talks with Red Cross personnel in Nevada. Source: FEMA Photo Library

Federal employees monitor a practice disaster during an exercise. Source: FEMA Photo Library

result of constructive experience.

To support broader learning and innovation, FEMA will realign and enhance existing and emerging training and education programs for state, local, tribal emergency management officials, and FEMA employees, into a comprehensive emergency management curriculum. FEMA's Emergency Management Institute (EMI), Center for Domestic Preparedness (CDP), and the FEMA-sponsored Center for Homeland Defense and Security (CHDS) at the Naval Postgraduate School will play prominent roles in this effort. The programs at EMI, CDP, and CHDS, along with FEMA's other training and education providers, will serve as the basis for training in core competencies across four areas; foundational, technical, management and leadership. FEMA's approach will emphasize education opportunities for newly appointed emergency managers and staff from state, local, tribal and territorial, and Federal emergency management offices. It will focus on the core competencies to provide new practitioners with broad and generalized knowledge and skills in the field of emergency management that meaningfully correlate to job performance. It will also build on executive level programs that build strategic leadership competencies and foster collaborative action among current and future emergency management leaders.

FEMA will create structured mechanisms, including establishing an innovation council, to promote and enable development of creative solutions to emergency management challenges. We will create opportunities to bring together leading entrepreneurs, technologists, academics, stake-holders, and subject matter experts from diverse fields to offer fresh perspectives and alternative approaches. We will also continue our efforts to understand the future environment and develop strategies that will allow the emergency management community to address upcoming needs.

The best ideas, whether generated internally by FEMA employees or through a synthesis of collective brainstorming sessions and workshops, will help the national emergency management team adjust operating concepts and approaches. By doing so, the team will be able to achieve more effective outcomes and enhance the Nation's resilience to disasters. FEMA will foster an innovative culture that accepts and integrates fresh ideas to resolve longstanding challenges, encouraging FEMA employees and our partners to examine a situation, apply a broad set of shared experience, and make decisions that are in the best interest of the American people.

Enhancing Learning and Innovation

FEMA will seek to promote learning and innovation at the Agency and throughout the emergency management community by:

- Promoting original thinking by empowering individuals to think "outside the box"

- Creating doctrine to guide and improve data collection, analysis and sharing

- Leveraging real-world and exercise data to create new approaches to training and planning

- Conducting emergency management innovation workshops

- Enhancing Emergency Management Institute (EMI) and Center for Domestic Preparedness (CDP) training programs

- Conducting outreach to non-emergency management personnel to obtain an alternative view

Figure 7—Learning and Innovation

Key Outcomes to Achieve

- Create a collaborative infrastructure to support learning and innovation across the emergency management enterprise

- Establish an integrated after action process that consistently evaluates operational performance both in real and simulated events, probes how underlying community conditions contribute to disaster impacts, and tracks Agency-wide efforts, working with our partners, to act on and address lessons learned

- Establish an innovation council within FEMA to promote and enable development of creative solutions to emergency management challenges

Evaluating and Managing Performance

★ ★ ★

Federal Agencies in general and FEMA specifically, are under greater pressure to demonstrate that they provide tangible results to the public within a constrained fiscal environment. We must improve our focus on producing results that benefit the public, and also must give the public confidence that FEMA has produced those results.

For the last several years, FEMA has been working to strengthen its Budget to Performance Integration (BPI). The objective of BPI is to enable leaders to look across the activities that FEMA performs and determine whether the organization's resources are being optimally used to achieve our mission. Other public organizations, such as the New York City Policy Department, the City of Baltimore, and the Department of the Treasury have developed new performance frameworks that facilitate the conduct of systematic discussions about the performance of their organizations. These data-driven management systems are designed to monitor and improve performance in real time using data-tracking and management tools, many of which FEMA already uses (e.g. performance tracking and geographic information systems mapping software).

Beginning in Fiscal Year 2011, FEMA will implement a new performance improvement system, FEMAStat, modeled on these approaches (Figure 8). This new approach will enhance integration among FEMA's strategy, budget, and personnel resources, and performance management processes, and to demonstrate the outcomes being achieved through Agency activities meaningfully. As part of this system, FEMA will establish a new, formal performance review process, and will require development of annual operating plans for all headquarters elements and Regional offices. These new

Managing Performance

FEMA will employ a performance-based management process based on the successful New York City model, which will be called FEMAStat. As part of this process, FEMA will hold an ongoing series of frequent, integrated meetings during which principal members of the FEMA leadership team, including the Deputy Administrator, as well as the top managers of different FEMA components and regions will use current data to analyze specific, previously defined aspects of past performance in each functional area. The regular meetings will allow leadership to provide feedback on progress in achieving outcomes; to follow up on previous decisions and commitments to produce results; to examine and learn from each program's efforts to improve performance; to identify and solve performance problems; and to set and achieve new performance targets.

Figure 8—Managing Performance

mechanisms will allow FEMA to better evaluate how it is employing its resources in support of its strategy, the outcomes being achieved through the deployment of those resources, and the effectiveness with which these outcomes are being achieved. FEMAStat will also provide the means by which FEMA will assess, on an ongoing basis, the implementation of this strategic plan. FEMA is committed to operating transparently and to evaluating its performance consistently in a manner that ensures accountability and improves both service delivery and mission effectiveness.

A FEMA trainer answers questions during a break at a Joint Field Office in Wisconsin. Source: FEMA Photo Library

FEMA employees work together, and with partners, to improve the performance of the Agency. Source: FEMA Photo Library

Conclusion

★ ★ ★

FEMA recognizes that, as an organization and a member of the broader emergency management community, it must continue to evolve and adapt if it is to fulfill its mission successfully now and in the future. The FEMA 2011-2014 Strategic Plan builds on the progress FEMA has made to date to create a stronger organization contributing to a more capable emergency management community. This Plan is focused on four initiatives that will better enable FEMA to work with partners nationwide to create a more effective emergency management enterprise. First, FEMA will support broader engagement with all segments of our society to enhance preparedness, security, and resilience and foster a community-oriented approach to the practice of emergency management nationally. Second, FEMA will work with our partners to build the capabilities necessary for all members of the Nation's emergency management team to facilitate the response to and recovery from catastrophic events. Third, FEMA will facilitate development of a common understanding of the risks we face so that together we can collaborate to prioritize the development of capabilities and unify efforts to address them. Finally, FEMA will improve the services it delivers and outcomes it achieves by enhancing the Agency's ability to learn and innovate. These initiatives are tied to the overarching concepts of preparedness, resilience, unity of effort, and team. They are linked to one another and

Administrator W. Craig Fugate and American Red Cross President Gail McGovern sign a memorandum of agreement to provide mass care after a disaster. Source: FEMA Photo Library

are the foundation from which new innovations, concepts, and approaches for emergency management can be built. Success of the FEMA Strategic Plan, like the success of all FEMA activities, is dependent on the full engagement and support of the entire emergency management community. This plan is bold, but necessary, and we are committed to continuing to reshape FEMA and enhance the practice of emergency management in the United States in order to ensure the security and resilience of our Nation and meet the needs of the American people before, during, and after a disaster.

www.ingramcontent.com/pod-product-compliance
Lightning Source LLC
Chambersburg PA
CBHW080942290526
45795CB00007BA/2857